To Linda

In the spirit of poetry

# *Typicity*

( 85 Poems! ) *fpl.*

## Colin Pink

Best w.

10 April 2021

**Typicity**

© Colin Pink

First Edition 2021

Colin Pink has asserted his authorship and given his permission to Dempsey & Windle for these poems to be published here.

Author photograph and front cover design by Caroline Kerslake.
Front cover based on *Icarus Suite II* etching and aquatint 2011
©Massimo Danielis

Published by Dempsey & Windle
15 Rosetrees
Guildford
Surrey
GU1 2HS
UK
01483 571164
dempseyandwindle.com

British Library Cataloguing-in-Publication Data

A catalogue record for this book is available from the British Library

ISBN: 978-1-913329-37-2

Printed in the UK by Imprint Digital (Exeter)

*for Jenny*
*and in memory of Irene and Ernest Pink*

Also by Colin Pink

*Acrobats of Sound*
(Poetry Salzburg Press, 2016)

*The Ventriloquist Dummy's Lament*
21 villanelles with 21 woodcuts by Daniel Goodwin
(Against the Grain Press, 2019)

**Acknowledgements**

Acknowledgements are due to the editors of the following publications where some of the poems first appeared: *Poetry Ireland Review; Acumen; Poetry News; Under the Radar; Magma; Poetry Salzburg Review; South Bank Poetry; American Writers Review; Orbis; Ver Prize Anthology; New Contexts 1 Anthology; Poetry Space Prize Anthology* and online at *The High Window; Ink Sweat & Tears; London Grip; The Blue Nib, Ekphrastic Review,* and *The Shot Glass*.

Thanks also to all those who have supported me in my writing by reading drafts, sharing their thoughts and suggestions and giving encouragement.

# Contents

## Hymn to the Thames

You are always moving, restless, changing your appearance,
        as if you can't decide what mood you're in.
Your inky skin covers over the dark thoughts of the drowned.

Your currents hurry up and down, always late for an appointment,
        giving lifts to fish working their way upstream,
who nestle in eddies, waiting for the tide to turn for the up escalator.

Along your shore beachcombers search for ritual offerings,
        gifted to you long ago, freighted with hopes
by now long fulfilled or not according to your will or whim.

Eliot for one believed a river is a strong brown god, but fallen
        on hard times, now just a problem, in the way
like the homeless. We pass you by and often fear to hold your gaze.

You glint at hidden depths, spawn stories, fish, and dead bodies.
        Your waves are restless sleepers always changing
position in perpetual search for contentment, drenched in dreams.

You were our first highway, a rapid gateway of commerce, a vein
        pumping nutrients into the nation's body, along
with other illicit substances, opiates to lull the nerves of the city.

You are a churlish friend, flooding the tow-path, strewing it with
        tangled twine and plastic bottles, reminding us
that all we have thrown away might come back to taunt us some day.

# Graffiti Triptych

## Beach

Someone had drawn a mermaid in the sand. I thought it
a good likeness and took a photograph with my phone.
Nearby the tide had deposited the malodorous gift
of a dead fish. But the mermaid didn't mind. Soon the sea
would return and lick her hair clean with repeated
strokes from hesitant but persistent incoming waves.

## Banksy

A little girl releases a red balloon. Each day I'd go past,
on my way to work, and there she'd be, releasing her
red balloon. Reaching up to the sky, away from the dry
grey steps. It cheered me to see her, always occupied
in lifting our collective spirits. I vowed to ignore any
irony that might be implied, preferring the spirit of hope
that pulsed from her diminutive figure and the red
balloon, which reminded me of a charming song.
One day, as I passed, a council worker was busy
noisily sandblasting her off the face of the earth.

## May 1968

*Sous les pavés, la plage…* Sometimes,
walking across Camber Sands with my
sneakers filling with grains – and the wind
casting fragments into my eyes I wish
there was beneath the beach a pavement.

**Hotel: Corsica Points the Way**


There's a stain on the carpet in the shape of Corsica.
It looks like a hand with a stubby finger pointing
along the corridor in the direction of the lifts. Is it
tea? Wine? Vomit? Perhaps a queasy geographer
passed this way or a clumsy worker whose room
service skills are still in their infancy. This corridor
is endless. Every door blanks me as I search for my
room. I'm sure I left it here somewhere. I might have
passed it the first time around and decide to double
back. Every room seems to hold its own mystery,
a container for a different person's history, which
sadly, I'll never unearth, their treasure undisturbed.

**Room 212**


This room could pass for a cell, except for the TV
on the wall opposite the bed. I'm self-condemned
to solitary, my condition eased by the distraction
of the mini-bar and switching channels, in faint
hope of finding something to watch less soporific
than my thoughts and less alarming than my fears.
The couple in the room next door seem to be having
a lot of fun or else they've found the porn channel.

Stale breath marinates in the air-conditioning which
emits professional moans. I think of that play by Sartre
where a hotel room stands in for hell. The view from
my window, which prudently won't open, presents
a panorama of overstuffed paladin bins, assaulted
by vagrant seagulls collecting an evening take-away.

## Hopefully to Dwell

To dwell is to tarry, stop awhile and just be; be where we are:
perhaps in a dark wood or else alone on an empty strand –
from the one you can't see far, the other stretches farther than hope.

The original meaning of 'dwell' was to make a fool of or lead
astray, like a magician or hypnotist who enchants us to our
cost and leaves us to rue the day we were made to dwell.

In Middle English 'dwell' meant to hinder or delay, like traffic
or the wrong kind of snow that makes a simple journey into
a vexatious string of uncertainties replete with privations.

The present sense of 'dwell' dates from the mid-thirteenth
century, so it's been around, sticking with us, staying put.
Dwell likes itself just as it is, no fancy footwork required.

**Trampled Earth**

We tore up the flowers, plucked feathers
from the birds to wear them in our hats.

We set fire to the forest to feed our passion
for meat, nourish investors' need for profit.

We praised how much progress we made
speeding ever faster to the end of the road.

**Face Time** *(for Fritz)*


Good morning face! Old friend.
We're looking a bit bristly. Time for a shave.
We've been together for a long time.
But know each other only in the mirror;
a reversal of what everyone else sees.
But it's how we meet and it helps a lot
when applying shaving foam and scraping
away those bristles with the razor, cutting a swathe
in the white foam like a dutiful householder
clearing snow from their path.

There now! We're looking smooth again.
At least around the lips and chin.
Though every time we meet in the mirror
it seems that someone has taken a line for a walk
and wrinkles have grown by stealth. As for
the bags under our eyes, what was once just
carry-on luggage will soon need to be checked-in.
Good morning face! Old friend.
The sun is out and the birds are singing.
We are ready to face another day.

**Façades** *(for Gordana)*

The architecture of dreams has no ground plan;
the lifts make up the floors as they go along
and no one remembers their address any more.

Many buildings are destined to be designed, few built,
their blueprints the smudged mascara of long nights;
and all façades hide the fact they're hiding something.

But the soul of the architect peeps from the windows;
the bone structure of faith gives a certain beauty
to every building no matter how bruised by time.

## Appearance and Reality

The fly raps smartly on the window, like a rent
collector who cannot believe that no one is in.

It hurls its body again at the invisible barrier
that keeps both hope and frustration alive.

Dauntless, it turns itself into a hammer to crack
the pane and regain the freedom of open air.

The glass will not give and an angry buzz
vibrates through it but still there's no way out.

It pauses awhile, contemplating this puzzling turn
of events, as it waits for energy to hurl itself again.

Later, I see it, quiet at last, a black speck, wings transparent
against the light, at the foot of the sill — the window open now.

**The Problems of Philosophy** *(after Bertrand Russell)*


The table I write at appears solid, smooth and polished;
reflections of light glow white on its surface. If I turn
my head the colours change, the highlights skate across
the top; one edge looks longer but isn't. Depending on

your point of view it all looks different. To the painter
these things are important. Russell's elegant prose claims
we always experience a veil of appearances, never reality;
and to make it sound scientific he calls it 'sense data'.

That world seems to be reliable, dependably the same,
tomorrow as it was today. And yet, we're like chickens
who everyday are fed by the farmer at the same time.

But one day instead of feeding the chickens he wrings
their necks. This is known as the problem of induction.
Not a lot of chickens know that. And neither did I.

## Vague Intimations of (Im)mortality *(after Wordsworth)*

Yet there you appear on the farther shore
not waving but welcoming all the same
fading in and out — a phlegmatic signal.

Your new form barely drawn on the air
a vague outline hardly divisible from
the haze that cloaks all expectations.

You slip through a narrow casement riding
a tightrope of light not trailing clouds of glory
but floundering in a sanguine faecal delta.

Shipwrecked on a sheet with a squall of air
bursting from your lips rudely tugged from
this doughy loam — a choleric human clay.

Prison walls close-in erected by well-meant
hands whose clumsy artifice moulds your
nascent form into misshapen possibilities.

Melancholy mirrors are placed before you
funhouse distortions of all the projections
thrown onto your own fragile story-line.

Paradise is a taste half-remembered barely
encountered as you journey from first step
to last, carrying always Pandora's final gift.

## Bon Anniversaire

First cry, slicked in mother blood, licked in mucus,
shining and matted, pain-filled and triumphant,
greeting the dawn in which your days are birthed
your soul earthed to this time and no other. Every
breath thereafter leaves a trail, silvering across
your skin's calendar like a snail. Winter's hoarfrost
breath, spring's eager buds and showers, summer's
sweaty fructification, autumn's vespertine matings.
Year on year entirely the same and entirely different.

Random encounters range before you and recede,
double back, among mountain tracks, false starts
as the grip of memory gradually slackens. And you:
always adding up, parsing for sense. Before the light
of reason strikes a shadow falls and wipes the board.
Steady on the tiller, through calms and rapids, prey
to a sudden vertigo let slip by nature's palsied grip.
Still searching the horizon for a safe shore when you
hit that final drop and the world turns flat after all.

## Spade Lines

Running forward looking back
with my handful of years I trail behind me
a miniature spade – leaving a long line in the smooth sand.

I enjoy making marks on the land
loop the loops whose burred edges inscribe a nascent
handwriting – spring flowers blossoming after a harsh winter.

## Spur Bridge Mortlake

Standing, bow taut, on the Spur Bridge that spans the urban
railway line, and stretches up, a wrought iron cat arching
its back, to accommodate carriages that thunder below,
steel wheels on steel rails, charging onwards with implacable
urgency. I remember you, I remember you; you were both
scary and beautiful. As a child I climbed your wide spaced
steps and peered through gaps in the treads at clinkers
far below and felt the sharp nudge of vertigo at my back.
Mum spat words to make me hurry. But I feared to fall
into that maw and be swallowed whole before I got across.
Gazing down at the dizzying ground I'd grasp hold of your
cold ungiving arm and be so glad to land on the other side.

**The Ascent of Everest** *(for Malcolm)*


At school we were made to read *The Ascent of Everest*.
Possibly one of the dullest books in the universe.
Written by a man who knew a lot about climbing
but nothing about telling a story. It was set for 'backward
children' designed to inculcate hard work and endurance
in those predestined for unskilled labour. It was guaranteed,
single-handed, to put us off reading for life. Forced to read
about traipsing from one 'col' to another was so tedious
it made us long for frostbite to escape the next chapter.

**An Open Book**

In RE the teacher marched through the class throwing
Bibles onto our desks. Battered 'thou shalt nots' thudded
one by one towards us, a rolling barrage, shocking as a
board rubber hurled across the room. Embodied unease
quickly passed, like childhood disease, from hand to hand.

These Bibles were illustrated with pictures filched
from the common store of religious art. I flipped
open my copy and the leaves parted at a drawing
of praying hands, rendered in silverpoint, the fingers
barely but tenderly touching. It is not Dürer's drawing

I remember but an anonymous artist who improved
the image in blue ballpoint pen, and rendered an erect
penis clasped between the open hands. It was a gleeful
slap in the face of piety. Sacred and profane slept
together between the sheets. I quickly closed the book

fearing the teacher would think me the illustrator.
Now, whenever I see that Dürer drawing I can't help
recalling that anonymous twelve year old's brutish art.
Maybe he is now a celebrated Brit-Art figure, his talent
to shock curated and celebrated, no longer given free.

## Circus Ghazal

In the playground we'd re-enact, with youthful ruckus,
sketches from Monty Python's Flying Circus.

At Easter we'd watch the exploitation of sad animals,
performing tricks for us, at Billy Smart's Circus.

In America, we're assured, everything is bigger so – OOO
Barnum & Bailey misdirect with a Three Ring Circus.

Through my youth I haunted bookshops in the Charing
Cross Road – seeking a revelation of the Human Circus.

John le Carré imagined the offices of the secret service –
to be stuffy bureaucracy in Cambridge Circus.

I struggled to learn to conform, bend the knee
to the absurd clowns in the Work Circus.

A kiss on the station steps; wrapped in arms of passion
made me fear to lose my grip on the Love Circus.

Let's choose a landmark for a secret rendezvous or two…
how about the statue of Eros in Piccadilly Circus?

International politics, executed through proxies, unravels
around the globe into a Cruel and Bloody Circus.

There is no net; sooner or later you know you must let go
the high trapeze — fall into the gaping O of the Circus.

**4' 33"** *(after John Cage)*

I used to listen to it regularly
in the dentist's waiting room.
It would always start slowly:
a gentle slither and flick
of magazine pages accompanied
by the counterpoint of the distant
ringing of a telephone. I always
waited with constricted breath
to the sustained high notes
of the dentist's drill that would
hang in the air shrill as Valkyries
advancing. The rhythm section
was provided by the urgent
syncopated beat of trains on the
railway line across the street.
But it always ended on the mezzo
*sprechgesang* of the dental nurse
'We're ready for you now.'

**New Perch**


We balance on the balcony like two Japanese cups
    on a high shelf — together — rim to rim
        perfect and fragile in equal measure.

A shingle of stars lies scattered across the sky;
    it takes a long time for their light to reach this far
        — like a thought that dawns too late.

As we gaze up we reconfigure the constellations,
    tracing ourselves, joining dot to dot, making
        new stories to grace this velvet night.

**Unfolded & Refolded**

Folded and refolded over numerous readings
the letter flimsys itself over; at its centre a line
of writing is rendered illegible in the crease.

A wrinkle of meaning escapes the reader, yet,
held in gentle hands, the paper quivers with
that long held expectation to be understood.

## Addicted

How do I count the very things that master me?
No abacus is wide enough to quantify or calculate
the debts that lurk in the shadows of my eyes.

With every breath I hold dear the gift of oxygen
but cannot keep it, always dissipate it, and gasp
at how vast the distance lies, expelled, before me.

Welcome! Come in. Do sit down. Allow me to pour you
a little something, my own recipe you know. Let's swap
libations, imagine love without trials and retributions.

A heart works hard, does it not? Eager drummer to the
rhythm of life, pacemaker of our dreams, our hopes, high
hat dancing at the sight of you coming through the door.

The tintinnabulations of love can deafen in an instant
can trample all the roses cultivated for some imagined
love object clothed in the elusive outlines of desire.

Have I told you I'm addicted? Where can I possibly begin?
Let's not bother with bureaucracy, rules, accountancy,
but spend each moment casually without any reckoning.

Okay, okay, I know you want to know the worst: truth and
nothing but; how I broke the baby's piggy bank and fed
the meter of my desire with every last shilling, last syllable.

But that was yesterday. I'm a new person today! Yes I am.
Addicted to everything as before: both the good and the bad,
the ugly and the sad, but above all: everything I cannot keep.

## No Prometheus

but still speared by the beaks of remorse.
Every action has an equal and opposite
reaction. Sparks that light the sky die
in flight; we never see where they land.
Every message in a bottle goes somewhere;
no fixed abode, bobbing on tides that always
know where they're going, without need
of address, no satnav, no GPS. Some days
hesitation takes root. Everything tilts a little
to one side at each breath; possibilities
expand and contract like a lung, a heartbeat,
an infant's fierce grip. One day we'll get all
our plastic ducks in a line, a cheerful yellow
fleet on manoeuvres. Adrift, a temporary
protrusion between earth and sky, sometimes
I feel cloudless, all fears curled, like an adder
basking in the sun, just a naked footstep away.

**No Signal** *(a poem for two voices)*


*they say a letter always reaches its destination*
you drive and talk on the mobile phone
I try to discern your tone while the signal
wavers about like an old transistor radio
*perpetually re-directed much time may elapse*
your words blur my mind and meaning
crumbles in the sudden gaps that open up
as you travel our connection unravels
*they say if you cannot say it put it in a letter*
a breadcrumb trail that ends in a holzweg
a dead-end path as I speak I lose faith
in the weight of my own familiar words
*carefully folded into the crevice of an envelope*
whose dry flavour is lost in translation
every intersection replete with scepticism
we talk over each other clumsy dancers
*languishing in the heart's dead letter office*
stepping on each other's words no beat
no natural rhythm no sense of recompense
addressing questions no longer relevant
*the peaceful repose of unopened letters*
but unable to stop talking or to accept
the comfort of silence as we climb
a swaying peg-ladder of words
*tied with red ribbon in a drawer*
it is so wonderful to live
in an age of instant
communica

## Choice Cuts

She cuts herself into thin strips
and feeds them to the wolves.

Each day she does it again
and they are always hungry.

I howl, my tendons vibrating
in sympathetic harmony.

Pneuma of hope, one exhalation,
one jump of the heart.

She regenerates after butchery
in order to torture herself again.

Her cunning mind is scalpel sharp
surgically removing our ligaments.

I am helpless as a dismembered
torso, my every move stumped.

At night she hangs her carcass
on a hook, ready for the next day.

## Just out of Sight

You were stroked by every mirror you walked past;
invisible hands reached out to caress your shadow
but were always too late to touch the hem of beauty.

There was always something just out of sight, lost
to peripheral vision, never quick enough to catch
a visitant who possessed the answers to questions

we struggled even to formulate. Questions that
followed us, like a lame but faithful dog, pausing
only to sniff at possible solutions deposited by others.

There was something pagan in your walk, comfortable
with the earth beneath and the sky above, even when
it's clothed in tarmac or obscured by obelisks of power.

Shop windows and the slick bodywork of automobiles
stared back at you in disbelief, unable to blink or turn
away. But these reflections always had nothing to say.

Were you a mirage of desire everyone could see but no one
could grasp? Your limbs returned everyone's fantasies with
interest but the capital sum of your self remained untouched.

Crossing roads, against the light, the traffic bowed down
before you, temporarily frozen and forgetting any sense
of destination. Zebras cherished the touch of your foot.

The city opened its doors like so many arms making
gestures of welcome. The excited apertures of camera
phones expanded but you were always just out of focus.

**Above My Head**


Footsteps in the flat above. The creak of floorboards
flexing with the weight of someone I've never met,
their existence surmised by sound. What's going on

up there? My mind drifts, like a helium balloon up
to the ceiling, bobbing in curiosity. Thud of furniture,
laughter, then sudden shouting. Is it an argument

or some kind of noisy love play? Both might create
this spate of thuds and bumps, rend the air with
the vigour of their enactment. Something breaks.

Hurried feet, the slam of a door, the thunder of steps
raining down the stairs; the hasp of company becomes
unfastened. The building settles down like a dog resting

its head on its paws. Silence returns. The air feels lonely
as an abandoned shoe. I think of footprints and remember
snowy days. I'd make crystalline imprints in fresh snow:

my steps leaving a trail of clues — proof I really exist.

**Incarnated**


Now that you are nowhere I find you everywhere.
You whisper in my ear when I least expect it. I see
your face in my mirror, hear your voice in my words.

And look, you've even inhabited my lopsided smile.
When will it be time for us both to take a break?
I know you won't say. I never took your advice

and you never gave it. How wise you were. I didn't
notice at the time, mistaking silence for stupidity.
I was always too slow on the up-take and still lag

behind after all these years. Every witty riposte
lands on my tongue too late. First thoughts are
often forgotten, too fleet or cunning to be caught

in the snare of language; second thoughts are paltry
seeding confusion in a mind overgrown with the
invasive weeds of others' ideas. So many voices,

each insists it is right, but tonight there is no debate
just the long open arms of love, stretching, stretching,
stretching, so patient, waiting for us to run into them.

## View from the Studio Dresden


Stare out the window, breathe and watch
the Elbe float by. Gilded dreams rise
to the surface, flash briefly up, then sink.

Casements fillet the view, frame reality
like a picture that won't be contained
will always spill over vision's edge.

The shadows speak to me, creep across
the wall, fingers searching for something
misplaced long ago that remains in memory.

Every second everything changes, depending
where you look. Regard this oak's ridged bark,
and look at this granite rock, its fissured skin.

Lost in a crevice filled with pungent shadows
I can see further with my mind than my eyes
but no compass can tell me which way to go.

Nothing preserves these moments, bidden
or unbidden, their sudden bite, like stubbing
a toe. Hush, hush, let nothing fill your brush.

When I run to tell my story nobody's home.
Stare long enough at a blank wall and it fills
with the stain of all things, scars plastered over.

At this time of day light falls in such a way
it carves up the floor and ceiling with geometric
precision, dividing everything into light and dark.

Place your hand across the divide, let it be cut
in half, neither one thing nor the other, crossing
the border between the luminous and numinous.

## On Not Being Able to Pray

In a dingy church in a foreign town, whose name
I've forgotten, I lit a candle; drawn by the flames,
even though I don't believe, I lit a candle for you.

It must be the atmosphere of this place, a theatre
of holiness, diurnal rituals, that conjures a nugget
of faith, wrapped in hope, from my agnostic soul.

The stones around me are soaked in prayer. If I touch
them I feel the vibration of a holy longing preserved
within. Many lights gleam before the altar and spill

their tiny hopes onto an ugly metal tray. As pious
gestures go it's easy, cheap, no wonder so many
set these small offerings, soon to be snuffed out.

All that's left is a stubborn pool of cold candle grease.
Though I'd like to pray instead I turn my back and head
for the door into a brighter and harder light than before.

## Relics' Requiem

Behind glass, resting now, as after a long
journey, putting their feet up, the relics
are checked-in to the cathedral treasury
like so many tourists in a mid-range hotel.

Formerly they were carted from place to place
like family heirlooms, by monks and priests,
stolen like silver or gold credit cards to heaven
by pilgrims, invaders and rival orders. What

is that absurd need to eff the ineffable that
drives us mad? Here it is: masquerading
as fragments of bone; vials of dried blood;
foreskins. How dreary they look shucked

from their shells: dirt under ancient finger
nails; the itchy aroma of dust; the shrivelled
skin of hope, dry and wrinkled as a face
whose beauty has been capsized by time.

The relics keep their secrets, snigger at our
confidence in the capacity of the intangible,
Laugh Out Loud at our longing for the
numinous to blunt the blade of the real.

## Funeral for a Friend

There were photos of you everywhere at your funeral
perhaps to distract us from the fact you were in that wicker casket.

And people talked and talked about you, how good you were,
as if to distract us from the fact you could no longer talk.

They would keep talking about your work, when your work
was the last thing on my mind, as if this was a retirement 'do'.

And then we walked out into the rain, relieved to be away
from all the talk, and we walked into the forest where nature

might apply its arnica to our bruised souls, as we walked slowly,
uphill, with our burden of memory getting heavier and heavier.

And then we came to a hole in the ground and, bizarrely,
they were going to put you into this hole in the ground.

And it was only then that I was hit by the stark realisation:
it was just a hole in the earth and they were going to put you in it.

As if you were being punished for hiding away from us and not talking
any more. And after an awkward pause they lowered you down.

And then we all filed past and dribbled handfuls of earth onto you
as if making a libation, as if giving some kind of leaving present.

But there was no gift in it because you would not be sprouting
in the spring, your smile blossoming, fresh as a daisy.

Then we went back to the Centre and being English drank tea;
though frankly I could have done with something stronger.

And we ate a surprising amount, as if to fill a void bigger than hunger.
And we talked as if to fill a silence that was too painful to listen to.

I remembered, when we were at university together, asking you:
What's your favourite thing? And you said — *Sleep, falling asleep.*

And now, one year later, my macabre mind can't help wondering
what it's like down there, in your hole in the ground in the forest.

Reality pulls an ugly face it's unwise to gaze at too long. I tell myself
you've gone on a long holiday and have forgotten to send a postcard.

## Irene and Prince

Irene is eighteen and looks like a movie Queen;
her Clara Bow lips rouged for an adoring kiss
in the final reel. Prince, the Alsatian, stands alert,

ears pricked, leash held gentle in his mouth,
a happy canine captive to his mistress. Irene's
sleek summer dress, wide brimmed hat, worn

aslant, and white gloves, are straight from a style
magazine. Prince's glossy coat, taut haunches
and alert ears are a fitting accessory to her Holly-

wood wardrobe. Behind them the trees mask
the horizon. The future is just out of sight
couching in the dark wood. Prince aims his

questioning gaze straight at the viewer, like a
bullet, suspicious of the intent of the man behind
the camera. Irene's life will soon become a movie

more dramatic than she planned. And though
she stands, auditioning for a romance, all the while
the hidden scriptwriters, far away, labour night

and day on a different story, an epic war picture.
Prince looks out and his sharp doggy gaze is wise
beyond her years. He smells the plot unfolding.

Who is behind the camera? Her father took the shot,
wielding the box-brownie like a weapon, freezing time
for just this instant. Later he had the dog 'put-down'

claiming it was dangerous. Her mother said it was
because the dog disliked her father's mistress;
so that was the end of appeasement. And yet,

behind the photo's shiny surface, Irene and Prince
stand in perfect harmony, a glamour couple,
about to walk down the long red carpet of life.

**Triptych**

**Final Words**

You summed it up, as you lay on the bed,
when you said: *I don't know what to do.*

Neither did I. There was nothing to be done;
that was the problem. Solutions come to an end.

Every rung of the ladder is another painful step
but yet, once ascended, all we can do is let it go.

**Mother's Bed**

Afterwards, they came and dismantled the bed.
It was special and could tilt in any direction;

you could lower it all the way to the floor. Now
they've packed it away it seems surprisingly small.

As they carried it out to their van it reminded me
of when the undertakers came and took you away.

**My First Birthday**

It was my first birthday after you died.
I was one card short. And felt strangely alone.

After all, your birth is a memorable event
for your mother too, not easily forgotten.

Now I'm taking some fresh tottering steps
into a world without that familiar safety net.

**Rewind**


I'm looking into a neat hole in the ground
at your little bag of ashes and my gaze is so strong
that it levitates into the air like a drone.
It flies up and away from this Somerset cemetery
and follows the M3 back to London.
It hovers over Hanworth crematorium, swoops
into the furnace and sucks up the flames
reconstituting skin, muscle and bone.
And your body reappears on your bed
where your last breath re-enters your lungs
and kick starts the bellows of life.
The marrow in your bones regenerates
nourishing your blood with stem cells.
Your eyesight too returns from the shadows.
Your leg, divorced from your body for ten years,
regrows with no pain. The agony of gangrene
no longer gnaws at your flesh; it's sucked back into
itself, turning from black ooze to pink skin.
And your veins unclog so the blood can surge
through you, like a spring tide, up and down
your limbs. And you hop back like a sparrow
from a narrow pier at San Marco onto a speedboat
as if all your years weighed nothing at all.
And you keep on going, racing through time,
getting younger and younger every year
until you are born again.

## Swiss Army Knife

Now he is ninety he gives his grandson
his Swiss Army Knife. He must have
kept it for a long time. But it still works
perfectly. One by one he unfolds each
stubborn tool hidden within its neat body.

The corkscrew, the little saw, the bottle
opener, the screwdriver, the little pair of
scissors and a mysterious hook… Finally,
all the blades are open to inspection, bristle
like a porcupine, all present and correct.

The baton is passed on; and in this particular
masculine moment, of show and tell and the
giving of essential equipment, there is unspoken
a valedictory message tucked among the blades.

**The View from Greatstone** *(for Caroline)*


Breakfast on the beach at Greatstone — a flask of tea
and a fruit scone. It's December and the sea's a grey
seal relaxing in the swell. The wind couches, languid,
as the slow waves gently stroke the shore. The strand
is littered with coastal refuse — hightide's coughed up
mucus – water logged wood, plastic sheeting, frayed
rope and abandoned shells. The nuclear power plant
squats in the distance, discreetly pissing into the sea
and lanky electricity pylons stride across the marsh
walking steadily in a northerly direction. Wooden
palings, wearing mismatched gloves, salute dog
walkers, worm harvesters, wave watchers. The paling
cradles my back, as I gaze out into the distance where
Dungeness Lighthouse gives me a subtle wink, sharing
a secret that we both solemnly promise never to reveal.

**The Wanderers**


It's night and you're sitting
outside the tent
     drinking whiskey     s l o w l y
carefully     as if
    its viscid lips
      have some secret
    they might let slip     onto your tongue
a secret you might not remember
    in the bland light of morning
but tarries for now     a companion
     against the chill


    looking up at the sky
the Milky Way  is a wiper blade smear
    across the sparkling
      windscreen of the night
where everything revolves     at its own speed
    and you look up
      and keep looking
        until a shooting star
    a plunge of joy
streaks out     a spark
    thrown down   and   going out
     in one gesture

**The Prize**


Pale sentinel, full as a raindrop poised on a sill
I see you as a transient orb to scry the future.
Later a sabre, crescent sharp, a lopsided grin.
If you weren't there we'd have to invent you
to have something to long for just out of reach
but tantalisingly close. A light to guide us
through the night. A mystic pilgrim always
circling, casting spells on the tide, driving some
mad with the burning light of unreason.
Finally, you became a prize in a cold war race;
a trophy wife for the bloated ruler of the earth.

**Wrecks**


Buried deep in a Cornish cove rusted plates
from wrecks, semi-submerged, thrust up
from the crystalline sand.

Twisted beyond recognition, bitten by salt
and wind, these wounded metal skins
keep their stories to themselves.

Even the smallest pieces are too heavy to lift,
won't budge, immune to persuasion
from puny fingers and hands.

You could easily snag your foot or finger on these
aquatic beasts' fins, anoint their limbs
with drops of sacrificial blood.

A bright carmine meniscus, trembling with
the pounding of the sea, slowly dries
to a rusty hue.

One stormy day all the wrecks will awaken,
brush off their blankets of silt and sand,
reset their broken bones;

And sail away, resume their routine, forgetful
of journey's delay, checking bills of lading,
seeking destination.

## Summer Gales Sennen Cove.


Summer gales turn our tent into a drunken boat;
the canvas yaws, riding gusts that pull it about
like toddlers fighting over a toy, until I think
we'll surely sink, hull shredded, and crawl out
from under flapping waves of damp canvas.

We're battered senseless by the storm's invisible
blows whose racket is unrelenting, preventing
sleep or comfort with its all night club-clubbing.
The radio clings to a thin signal, rising and fading,
offering sips of orchestral succour while the rain

lands on the canvas like blows from a cat-of-nine;
it's enough to make us yelp and by the third day
we begin to take it personal, start to believe some
obscure nature God, offended by our unwitting
trespass, is out to teach us a lesson we won't forget.

## A Rural Idyll

What do you do in the countryside?
Why, you go for a walk, of course.

So you set off on a little excursion,
across the fields, along the lanes,

beside the streams where sunlight
dances to the rhythm of the rills.

It swells your breast in a warm glow
but then you turn a corner and almost

walk into them; they're suspended
from the lowest branches of a tree:

a rodent lynching, their matted bodies
turning gently in the breeze

their necks stretched taut, elongated
by the twine that attaches them

to their dangling place. And there
they hang like an angry warning

not to come this way again if you
should ever be in search of beauty.

**TQ E20 N74**

I lie back and gaze at the sky: its ever changing
face reflected in me. People come and go; I pay
no attention. Little ones throw bread for ducks,
toss stones at me; I feel nothing. I'm locked
behind ice, a scarred and cracked windshield,
opaque as a cataract. Spring promises hot
kisses, blows cool breezes, pockmarks me
with showers. Autumn brings stormy winds
to card ripples on my skin, but gifts to me
a thousand golden boats shaken from the sky.

## In the Forbidden Garden

In the forbidden garden flowers are open wide,
petals spread, demanding adoration, precarious
and ripe, consummate in earth black as caviar.

Nature unfurls like ink in water, slowly uncurls
its secrets, lays them before us for a moment,
then dissipates into a grey cloud of unknowing.

Buds of suspicion bloom in the garden of delights,
journalistic insects scurry away with the evidence
but leave the fruits of truth rotting on the vine.

Here you never know the time, aware only it is scarce
and porous, merging after, before and now, helical,
a convolvulus turning its limbs toward the sun.

Perhaps all utterance is contained in a drystone wall;
silent dentals clenched until they ache from holding
so many homeless, abandoned, rough edged words.

In her cell Julian writes that all will be well, she's filled
with a limitless quest to find the spirit of love within
everything, as ironic bird song interrogates the dawn.

## Imaginary Selenography

The need to know; to fill to the brim
our little cup of knowledge and reach
out beyond our grasp. To observe you
and peer around each libration in order
to see your mystery. To wrap our fingers
around your darkness, touch the coldness
of space that lies between us. I'm making
a map so I can feel your pockmarked skin
and judge how much you have been hurt.
I'll invent a name that tries to transcend
those temporal borders that hem us in.
Eternal, immortal, so that we might seem
a little less random, abandoned, alone.

Note: *Libration* is the term for the slight wavering of the Moon perceived by
Earth-bound observers.

55

**Looking for the Coast of Bohemia**

Looking back I realise I spent most of my time
searching for the coast of Bohemia. My charts
were faulty, my knowledge was just hearsay,
no geography corresponding to what I sought.

The journey was a long one and often fraught
with hazards I had not anticipated. I discovered
many places and learnt languages on the way;
although I never found the coast of Bohemia.

Even after conclusive reports that it didn't exist,
which convinced many, I never stopped looking.
Awake at night, sometimes I believe I can hear
waves breaking on her shore, coming ever closer.

**The Somnambulist**


To awaken and find life had become, all
at once, an ill-fitting suit of clothes — itchy,

threadbare, full of holes and indeterminate
stains – your beliefs unfashionable castoffs.

To see yourself pinned in that harsh film noir
light, interrogated by a glaring Anglepoise.

Sweating that guilty sweat, soaking through
your shirt, sticking to you like a confession.

To wake up and realise you had sleep-walked
through so much time – hardly any of it was left.

And still barely knowing what to do with it;
a gift you simply never learned how to use.

**Two Engravings by Albrecht Dürer**

**Vita Imaginativa**
(*Melancholia I*, 1514)

Brooding in the shadow of hubris, seeking glints
from the light of reason, absorption so entire
even the beauty of shooting stars can't compete.

The perpetual hum of thought; planing away at ideas,
aiming for smoothness so complete no critique can get
a grip. The handsaw of doubt rasps the mind, embeds

splinters of discontent and the itch of disappointment.
The magic square of longing always adds up the same
and equations are no comfort when burning in the flame.

The scales remain forever poised, balanced between
the elements, embroiled in a cacophony of theories,
the bell of divine revelation always remains unrung.

**Vita Contemplativa**
*(St Jerome in his Study,* 1514)

Unveiled. Like a blessing sunlight fills the room, illuminating
a clearing to the unconcealed. Gently, gently. Everything
listens to the scrape of Jerome's nib on the smooth vellum.

Unhurried. He writes slowly, brim with bright tranquillity,
bent to his task, his sure-footed pen paces the parchment;
ink glints a moment then births the Word into the world.

Untroubled. The room of contemplation breathes easily.
Everything is in its place. Welcome to the space of harmony,
embrace of certainty, where every mystery troubles no more.

Note: On his journey to the Netherlands Dürer frequently sold or gave away these two
engravings as a pair. According to Panofsky they contrast 'a life in service to God with what
may be called a life in competition with God – the peaceful bliss of divine wisdom to the tragic
unrest of human creation'.

**Making the Katana** *(a Samurai sword)*


First select the finest ore. Only
*tamahagane* – jewel ore – will do.

Wrap the *tamahagane* in a wet cowl
of Chinese drawing paper and birth
the steel in blue-white flames to turn
it golden. Scry the perfect heat within
the colour of the flame. The bellows will
breathe life into it, as trinity of hammer,
heat and quenching slowly shape it.

Score the skin with blade and hammer,
fold it over onto itself again and again
to exorcise impurities, until there is no
inside or outside: cross-wise and
length-wise hammered into one.

Melded together like lovers, hard steel
for sharpness, soft steel for resilience,
married in the sacrament of the blade.
The rhythmic tapping of the swordsmith's
hammer slowly draws out the supple curve
of the Katana's sinuous self. Ah Katana —

your shining body is painted in dull clay,
powdered stone and sifted charcoal,
heated and cooled to temper you.
With sharp little taps the swordsmith
incises his signature along your length.

The scabbard maker sheaths you in wood.
His chisel shaves the grain spinning out thin
curlicues, that decorate his thigh, as the wood
becomes a perfect hidden echo of your body.

Finally, you ride the whetstone, rocking your
brightness along it, absorbing the lightning
of your edge until you are sharper than
the rising Sun and in one gesture
can cleave the world.

**The Vision of Chancellor Rolin** *(after a painting by Jan van Eyck)*


Chancellor Rolin is on his knees before his prie-dieu.
He sees a vision of the Virgin and Child before him.
His gimlet eye assesses them, as if about to negotiate
a deal; reach some accord; strike a bargain with heaven.

Rolin knows many secrets, who can be bought and how.
That brocade gown cannot disguise his calculating heart.
Beyond the window the river purls toward the horizon.
This land profits him more than the peasants who work it.

As Chief Adviser to the Duke of Burgundy he knows
all the ways to manipulate with bribes and threats
in the court and market. His portrait is by the top
court artist; nothing but the best can purchase piety.

**Lepanto** *(after Cy Twombly)*

It's a wake of sorts: procession passing,
scrim of dream, blazon of nightmare.

The battle is over; all that's left scattered gifts:
driftwood limbs, blood stains diluted on the tide.

The wounded carry their wounds always, visible
and invisible, sharp as sea spray flung in the eyes.

The composite bow of time unleashes its quiver
of arrows in sudden and fearful velocity.

The ooze of history seeps between our toes
as the sea swirls up at the lip of the shore.

Rocks of longing and loss, wilder shores of love,
fill the horizon with boats, each its own sunset.

A stigmata of blisters blossoms on our palms, our
oars dipping, sparkles surfacing, fish leaping.

Rowing against the tide our strokes carry us
ever nearer to the elusive coast of Bohemia.

**All the Traces** *(i.m. Ana Mendieta)*


The shape of you is everywhere
But your shining self is nowhere
There is a Devil inside me you said
But the real devils are outside
Unseen hidden behind smiles
The tree of life will absorb you
It quivers in the storm of days
And the sky reflected in the water
Makes your body appear to float
Into the heavens a divine ascension
Except the mud you're made from
Brings all things down to earth
You huddle into the dirt as if
Snuggling into a mother's breast
Seeking tellurian sanctuary
In your exile there is nowhere
On earth you can call your own
But all the earth belongs to you
Invites you to caress it lie down
And measure the shape of your self
Within its embrace a tender self-burial
Welcoming so welcoming the soil
Land gentle fierce flame land safe
And open up all the roses on the
Same day at the same time all open
And the ribs of the day that hold you
Within the cage of time they will break
And must let you go let you go.

**Woodman Variations** (*i.m. Francesca Woodman*)


Always hidden in plain view, within yourself.
Under-exposed, over-exposed, always exposed.
Playing dead, among the roots, the undergrowth.
It's all an act, isn't it, running with the wolves?
Your body, your instrument, how you play it.
Get your knees dirty, stay close to the ground.
The Calla Lily's bold erection always beckons.
Flaking plaster, broken tiles, abandoned rooms.
Hide behind wallpaper, merge into the wall.
Crawl up to your reflection in deposed mirrors.
Scream, slash the walls; summon Rilke's angel.
Teach the glove to love the touch of fingers.
Be weightless, suspended before the door.
Thin arms so frail yet free as bird's wings.
Display your fishbone spine for us to strum.
Stroke the foxgloves; always keep their secret.

**Double Shelton Wet/Dry 1980** *(after Jeff Koons)*


They are immortal. They never change.
But the world around them moves on.
Clothed in pastel livery, once desirable,
now they look oddly quaint; their slick
bodies unblemished, they never go out.
They are immortal. They are never used
so they don't break down or wear out.
Such immortality is bought at a fearful
price: the cost of never living at all.

**Elisabeth Macke with Apples**
*after Portrait with Apples (Portrait of the Painter's Wife)*
*1909 by August Macke*


She comes from the dark bearing
gifts from behind a heavy curtain
whose soft folds echo her smile.

Red and russet apples balance
on a white plate held before her:
an offering to the God of still life.

Broad hands give us confidence
that nothing will slip from this
delicate yet perfect arrangement.

Her white shawl caresses her with light
bright as herself. Her eyes and lips
make three perfect almonds bracketed

by the calligraphy of her eyebrows
and chin. She looks down to her left
confident in the fruition of all things.

Moontide full she knows the touch
of brush, the smell of paint, the crunch
of apple, the repose of hidden seeds.

### Elisabeth Macke Reading

*after The Painter's Wife (study for a portrait) 1912 by August Macke*

She reads, absorbed in her book,
her body a lectern for thoughts.
Her head bowed as if in prayer
hands holding open the page.
The book balanced, precarious
wings, on the edge of the table.
She is a picture of concentration
and wisely disregards the clamour
of all the items that surround her:
the tablecloth, the fruit bowl and
oil lamp, that distract her husband.

**Confluence Point**
*after the painting by August Macke 1911*


His brush knows how it feels
to touch your skin and the joy
of surveying the topography
of your breasts and thighs
and everything between.
He paints you with such
love, a restrained eroticism
that makes me quiver to see
such openness, such manifest
togetherness, still unbroken.

Conscious of decorum he never
depicts the intimacies he knows.
Except one time in a landscape
he paints a long sun baked lane
that divides and the whole vista
lies splayed open before us
at the hot confluence point.

## Three Old Photos – 1918

### I

Finger hooked over the rim
of a white cup his eyes look up
head tied in white bandages
a badly wrapped present — bow askew.
Steel helmet perched on his stomach
dent in the crown recording where the bullet went down.
The medic views him through an undisguised
frown. Just one of many stretcher cases.
It could be any time any place.
It is not.

### II

Shell upon shell upon shell
lined up in anonymous rows.
Light trickles down the smooth
curves of metal casings
reflecting the sharp light
from the factory's glass roof.
Shell upon shell upon shell
aligned like crosses in a military cemetery;
chemicals in phallic steel coffins
handled tenderly by workers: mostly women,
boys, a few old men, immersed in the pungent
spark of death suspended within a cordite heart
waiting to explode beneath their grip.

## III

Spokes against the horizon
        thin wheels like hoops
rattle on the narrow road.

Balanced between – a stretcher –
        makeshift perambulator
no bedtime story, no goodnight kiss.

**Emily Dickinson**


One tiny room was large enough to contain the whole universe;
A little life, a sip of strong liquor, proved all that was needed.
A glint of love, folded within the page of a letter, was all it took
To conjure a song from the wren that cleaved the air like a bugle.

The shudder of distant battles set the dry grass quivering;
Disguised as sunlight it cast misshapen shadows on the wall.
Disembodied footfalls paused as they approached the door;
Cut flowers in a vase, severed from the soil, blaze then wilt.

We are the tiresome playthings that won't fit back in the box;
Our stuttering selves barely glimpsed, except perhaps in a dash –

## Mr Rothko in the Studio *(for Daniel)*

Smoke curls up from the tip of his cigarette
into the still air. Lazy ectoplasmic limbs drift
upward from a perfect cylinder of tobacco,
fixed between his fingers, like a stick of chalk.

He is very still and looks. Just looks. For the
longest time. He looks as if meditating on a
wall. Silence shrouds the studio which feels
like church, comfortless, demanding from each

supplicant something beyond their ability to give.
He looks through the layers of paint, reading destiny
in the entrails of art. Grabs a brush, scumbles pigment,
blurs the vision, to see beyond the edge of everything.

**One Night in Babylon**
*('Portrait of Count St. Genois d'Anneaucourt' by Christian Schad)*


Things fall apart; so let's dance while the money lasts;
listen to music, drink champagne, exchange aperçu.

The Count, whose titled name is as long as a freight train,
is trim in tux and immaculate cuffs, hands hidden in pockets.

His inscrutable eyes refuse to choose or comment on
the enduring attractions of his glamorous companions.

Who knows what's below his stiff collar and starched shirt?
But his guests' attire is designed to inflame every desire;

draped in chiffon that unclothes them more gracefully
than nudity, barely misting the curve of breast and buttock.

These courtesans' gunslinger glances are critically aimed
at each other and if looks could kill they'd both be dead.

The Count is poised between proclivities: the excitement
of his mistress or the enticement of a tempting counterfeit.

He imagines the delights on offer, contemplates alternatives;
but why choose? After all it's the 1920s; and anything goes.

**Without Screams**


Watching *Psycho* with the sound turned down;
the blonde has sex with a married man. She steals
the loot from a leering rube under the nose of her
weaselly boss. On the run it's obvious she has to die;
the genre needs a sacrifice to restore the order of things.

She has to be put in her place and the place is Bates Motel.
The blade shines with a painful gleam, rocks back and forth
in the maniac's hand, and poor Janet Leigh reaches out
toward us for something to hold onto. The shower curtain
bursts from its rail, blood swirls then curls down the drain.
We hold our breath; the celluloid stabs the screen 24 x a second.

**Poetry Terminable and Interminable** *(Ars Poetica i.m. Jack Spicer)*

the poem isn't over
    it tracks your every move
changes of address
    new jobs new friends
it's always on your trail
    at night it grips you tight
wraps itself around your hip
    fills your dreams with false memories
laughs itself to sleep
    the poem won't give up
there are butterflies in the poem
    of course there are
beautiful butterflies
    real ones symbolic ones
butterflies that secretly believe
    they are lost souls
seeking the taste of the perfect petal
    alighting on the mind
evading the hunting net of neurons
    the poem isn't finished
it deals from a crooked deck
    releases the wild horses
of long disguised desire
    tramples your careful garden
hangs on the note like Charlie Parker
    clinging to the cliff edge
it is the needle in the vein
    the viscous cling of spirit to the glass
the embrace that never parts
    riffing from one mind to another
smuggled through customs
    hidden in a bouquet of dendrites

levitating from one body to another
      the poem never rests
a command module
      taking off intent on return
to the mother ship
      a sunspot on the lens of the mind
a burnt cornea
      the poem never ends
it just pretends
      crowd surfing its way over the audience
skimming the surface tension
      of multiple reception
an interminable heavy metal drum solo
      an unfinishable riff
from a guitar hero
      a jazz solo with no resolution
stranded in a sonic elevator
      late for an appointment
with eternity
      with the scaffold of desire
the drop of the heart
      the fire in the veins
the electricity in the wire
      the dance of the deranged
the podium of false starts
      the poem is never over
even after you put it away
      its slim spine disappearing
slipping onto a shelf
      or left on the bus
or given to a friend
      still it flows around you
the poem never gives up

**Stelae** (*i.m. composer Elisabeth Lutyens*)

the blunt scythe
bruises the stalks
the shining blade
sharpens the mind

dancing on the lip of time
chimes with fresh designs
quiet pulses abating
with old reverberations

sudden shivers descend
plunging narrow streams
never stepped into before
and never out of since

pacing the stave of memory
spontaneous time signatures
a remembrance, leaping into
octaves of chronos

pluck the breath note
slap and stroke the string
unleash this inattention
fastened to the sound

bright disc of sound
illuminate the room
break open each stanza
then the shadows fall

sad notes stroked and broken
forsaken signs on the page
newly risen voices
knotted swollen knuckles

carry me up to the light
cave dwellers phantoms
tellers of mythos whose
shadows alert and burn

come, see me, come
find me, glance me
behind you within you
a faint trace in time

step, on step, on step
plucked from the night
follow a path that is
no longer there

shrill calls summon me
bitter tastes follow me
once was never enough
nothing could ever stop

small, tiny, lost, fogged
clear small clearing
light blazes a moment
fades into the next

what's that hammering
demanding to be let in
again and again importunate
tugging the sleeve of time

whistle and I'll follow
pace pacing behind you
leap ahead unexpected
fall into blind embraces

straight hair frames your
face deep furrows mark
the place of mourning old
sorrows and new tomorrows

thud thud thudding
without any answering
the beat without rhythm
accused of treason

memorial so tiny no one
will see it, step on the sacred
unable to compass it
cast from the light

soft, so softly soft
a quiet voice barely heard
whispers breath wraiths
that bristle the air

## Mirror | Mirror

There's a ghost in the mirror, just out of sight,
it's elusive and never gets caught no matter
how long you look; it hides behind the light.

You can hear it pacing to and fro, tap-tapping
searching for a crack in the back of your mind;
its breath mists the glass but it isn't speaking.

Its hollowed-out soul rattles in the night like
a smoker's phlegmy lungs. Cold laughter comes
from behind your shoulder off to the right.

It's got a weird sense of humour, cruel
and sly. It's promised to tell your fortune
but you can't trust it to play by the rules.

It occurs to you it might want to swap place;
you wonder what it's like behind the glass
gliding along with disembodied grace.

There's a silver lining behind every mirror
but it's hard to see lost in a fog of fugitive
thoughts and prey to the snares of error.

Feeling dizzy you grip the porcelain bowl
seized by an agonising retch of the self
and bring up the sour stench of your soul.

A chill runs through you and then you know
the swap has already happened. A fearful
feeling inside continues to grow and grow.

**Smoke & Mirrors** *(i.m. Alix Roubaud, photographer)*


The ghost in the photograph walks across the floor;
alone in her universe, no claims on her any more.

She searches an empty room, frozen in midstride,
for some mislaid thought she might've left behind.

Translucent as frosted glass, but pungent as smoke,
her gestures both hesitant and eloquent still evoke

a flickering pilot light that ignites a tensile memory
sealed within the glossy alchemy of photography.

The ghost in the picture turns away: a silent mourner,
custodian of a negative always awaiting exposure.

### Silueta – Ana Mendieta


Your homeless silhouette grew in surprising places:
from mud in Iowa, red petals in Mexico, carved out
of sandy cliffs in Long Island or made from weeds
and roots or shaped from clay. You're a muddy moat
filled with water or carved from ice. Sometimes your
hands are held up in holy surrender, other times
they're tight by your side, bound in your shroud.
You ritually buried yourself all over the place.
Like an atom bomb victim you left your shadow
on floors and walls. You became nature – growing
from whatever was at hand. You stayed an unwanted
child, exposed to the seasons' gradual decay. No trace
now remains of your silhouette, except in memories
preserved in photographic emulsion. Like family photos,
a reminder, for future generations, that you were here.

## Fragment from Atacama

In perhaps the driest place on earth a flake of bone
huddles into the dirt. I pick it up and imagine who
it was. What hopes, what dreams lay within this skull?
Which loved ones still wonder what became of you?
I mourn your anonymity, fragment of pulverised bone,
as if your death (I should say murder) is not enough
and your persecutors must murder death, obliterate
every trace that once there *was* a death, *your* death,
*this* death which I hold in my hand. Who'd believe
a prison camp held its grip on this parched land
with huts and wires and towers? Demolished now:
not even footings left to score its profile; there's just
the wind's echo, an anguished howl, almost human.

## Breaking the Talking Stick

Mouths beaten shut they took away your language. Banned
from speaking it you unlearned your speech for theirs. Every
word rife with consequence, you spoke the language of defeat.

Weightless without repetition, untethered from daily life,
your culture caught a wasting sickness. Mouths rusted shut
as words piled up behind lips swollen with a crust of blood.

A lone phrase might slip out, escaping dentals of denial, mostly
your tongueless words mouldered, lame, clumsy as stiff spigots,
and were forgotten by all but the very old or the very stubborn.

**Departures**

Fear squats across every border
Pisses hot and steaming into the cold silence of morning
Fear reeks in the heart of order

Gather your belongings — clutch them tight
Make the uncertain journey — break the grip of mourning
Gather your courage — chances are slight

Here the sky glows with phosphorous
Ignites the dust of nightmare — chokes the throat of hope
Here the sky stinks — tastes sulphurous

Shirts strung on taut washing lines
Wave their flayed skin — lonely and remote as hope
Shirts semaphore from hollow spines

Every departure signals a return
The foreign hearth a fragile home to which you cleave
Every memory a brand that burns

Trampled grass springs up bold as before
So many blades glisten — sever sorrow as they cleave
Trampled grass returns green and endures

## A Key from Palestine *(for Amjad)*

hangs from its hook, easily overlooked,
but always there. Its sturdy body retains
a dull metallic gleam although it's been
a long time since it was polished by a hand
or sank its teeth into a welcoming cylinder
in a door made by a preceding generation,
hung beneath a lintel under which so many
greetings took place. The key itself is now
well-travelled, from pocket, to jacket, to bag,
to refugee camp, and here to the house of exile,
where it hangs from its hook, gathering dust
and memories around itself. The key on the
hook waits to return and be useful once again.

Hold it in your hand.
You can feel that unhomed heart
beating, longing to return,
and be united with the door,
which may not be there any more,
in a homeland become
a No-land.

A solid door is there to keep out and keep in.
But when the homeland, on which it's hinged,
dissolves beneath it a door is transformed into
a tent flap waving in the wind. The generations
of certainty that opened and shut, opened and
shut it, over long years of leaving home in the
morning and returning home in the evening,
can no longer return, even if they keep the key
always ready, a mute instrument until the promise
of return is fulfilled, and the door, which may not

be there any more, admits them again. Only then will the key unlock all the hopes that linger so long in the homesick hearts of a dispossessed people.

## Beginning and Ending

The shabby boat flounders
a future life is crowning
the sea grips the mother's
body fierce as a birth pang
her cries are extinguished
by waves as she pushes
the baby out and the sea
embraces them both.

It smothers them in wet
kisses filling their mouths
and they go down to drift
in the aqueous dark — two
deep sea divers tied together
by their umbilical cord.

**Never Accept Words from Strangers**


*Did you pack these words yourself? Has anyone given you*
*words to carry for them? Have you left your vocabulary*
*unattended at any point in your journey?*

As they snap on the rubber gloves to probe,
persuade and intimidate you realise
you're costive with words that aren't yours.

Don't accept words from strangers
however well-meaning they appear.
Remember: *Cui bono? Cui bono?*

Remove their hand from your crotch/purse/mouth;
rip out their fake smiles with your teeth.
There's violence folded within everyday phrases:

*Take Back Control,*
     *Economic Migrants,*
          *Make* [INSERT NATION HERE] *Great Again.*


Note: cui bono = Latin phrase meaning 'who benefits'?

## International Panic

The news is bad, brings facts that twist our hopes awry.
The news is bad, brings
                sorrow repeated with ghoulish relish.
I'm distracted but try somehow to keep on doing things.

I wonder who adds up the cost and is it embellished?
I wonder who adds up
                and who's left out of the reckoning
but will pay in ways that no one counts in this mashup.

Who calls the tune that leaves the people panicking?
Who calls the tune
                as the fabric all about us breaks up?
I'm waiting for some answers; I hope they're coming soon.

We're all just waiting for the all clear signal to startup.
We're all just waiting
                as all about us spring flowers bloom
mocking our anxiety with their cheerful colours waving.

I think we're trapped in a medieval painting called a Doom.
I think we're trapped
                by sinister men in the wings waiting
to use this emergency. We'll wake to liberties kidnapped.

They'll clamp us down and prevent us from protesting.
They'll clamp us down
                with fear and force. We'll be wrapped
in rule by diktat, resistance defused, as democracy drowns.

Who will stand by at the wake, sombre and black capped?
Who will stand by
                    to defend the ideals we can't disown?
They'll wait in the shadows, cradle a future no one can deny.

## The Journalistic Questions

I asked the teachers what the lesson meant —
But the teachers only knew the lesson was hard.

I asked the soldiers who the enemy was —
But the soldiers couldn't see through their sights.

I asked the preachers where the prayers went —
But the preachers only knew what's in the prayers.

I asked the politicians when the storms would end —
But the politicians only knew a storm would begin.

I asked the gaolers how sore the locks felt —
But the gaolers only knew they opened and closed.

I asked the writers why they told their story —
But the writers only knew they had to keep telling it.

## Guide to the City of Truth

Welcome to the City of Truth; we hope you
enjoy your stay. Since all the lies in the world
weigh more than all the truth, we have been
obliged to build our city on lies. Truth is used
solely for ornament. It looks good in small
doses and distracts from the city's foundations.
Our citizens are content walking on the paving
of deceit but tend to stumble when attempting
to traverse the uneven surface of truth.
Our online markets — where every item is free
but the shoppers are for sale — are stocked
with nourishing lies pre-packaged and ready
to eat. You need to forage for the truth which
has to be soaked overnight before it is edible
and even then often takes a lot of chewing.
The truth is hard to swallow and even harder
to digest. By now many of our palates are so
confused we simply can't taste the difference.

**Typicity**


I learnt a new word today
from the label on a bottle of wine:
Typicity.
Or perhaps:
*Typicité.*
Clearly made for export
the label printed in French and English.
It says the wine is full
of tenderness and typicity
(*tendresse et typicité*)
which is a bit like how I feel
when I think about us.
According to the label this wine
crosses borders with audacity,
nobility and success.
Something denied many people.
Typicity is a tender little thing;
it distinguishes and identifies us.
And is the very thing borders
are designed to keep out —
under the delusion of keeping it in.
It takes audacity to cross borders today;
they strip us of any nobility
to examine our *tendresse et typicité.*
There is an art to crossing borders with success
let alone *noblesse*
and remain clothed in our confounding typicity.

**Suspicion**


I'd like to report myself to a member of staff.
I've noticed I've been acting suspiciously lately.
I want to leave my baggage unattended although
I have been warned it could be destroyed. Often
I fail to mind the gap between me and my country.
I've stopped believing the things I'm told on TV
and sometimes catch myself thinking for myself.
I keep reminding people the Daily Mail adored
Hitler in the 1930s. It's time I turned myself in.
Clearly, I'm a risk to myself and other people.

## Two Triadic Couplets for Shameless Politicians

### The Blatant Lie

Was propelled with the grace of a skier leaping
from the lip of a ski ramp. It hung in the pure air,

fearless; didn't care if everyone knew it was a lie.
For a moment I wanted to believe it as it skidded

to a halt before my open mouth. It just lay there,
brazen before us, pulsing with its own audacity.

### Domestos Bottle

You stand to attention, your neck erect, alert
like a warrior waiting for orders. Though made

of plastic your body suggests armour. You are
the invulnerable Norse God of the bathroom.

Your label says you kill all known germs dead.
Something about implacable certainty scares me.

## When it's Real You'll Know

I knew that everyone had become familiar with
the secret war when the sudden thunder spoke
and we all assumed it was a bomb going off.

And rain fell as if it had something urgent to do.
I touched your skin. Knock, knock, can I come in?
Border crossings are more hazardous than before.

All the neighbours had their fences blown down
in the same night, woke to see, whether curious
or not, what was always hidden from their sight.

The future is turning sepia; an old photograph
no one believes in any more; a future drained
of colour like an old friend with a fatal illness.

The flags are fluttering but not for me. They flutter
over uncomfortable alliances, communal bigotry,
chanting over town a noxious litany of new treasons.

Switch off the television; enough tragedy for one day.
I want instead to dream of something new. Something
no one told us to believe in; something good and true.

**Beautiful Lies**

Athletic bodies in motion in the cold
cinematic light of silvery black and white.

The discus thrower's torsion spins us out
from our world into a past made glorious.

The beauty of lies flames from the screen
dazzles better than dry and gritty truths.

Who wants to chew on the bitter vetch
of reality when fantasy is sweet to taste?

Let's seek warmth at the hearth of glowing
screens and their precise illusions.

The spade turns the soil, scooping out
a glisten of worms — naked to the air.

Birds gather, flint beaks glinting,
inviting themselves to the feast.

Pity the carrion that cannot die quick
enough and must suffer its flesh hooked

By ravenous beak and claw, too weak to
protest as their innards are ransacked.

It's a chill wind that tugs at our cover
stories leaving our pale lies unearthed.

## Lucifer

When he turned up he was well-groomed and handsome,
just like I'd imagined him, looking something like David Bowie
in his *Thin White Duke* phase.

He pulled on my shadow like an overcoat and it was a good fit,
though it masked the elegant tailoring of his form; here and there
I still glimpsed a tail and horns.

He's a smooth talker but there is something unnerving about him.
It's true he has the best tunes; I wanted to hear his side of the story;
it wasn't easy being the smartest angel.

Think of all that frustration, with a boss like God. It would be
enough to make anyone want to stir things up and it's true
we're always crashing in the same car.

We stayed up late listening to his favourite tracks. I must admit
I was beguiled by his stories; he knew a lot of famous people
and made them sound charming.

The more he talked I realised his ideas were my ideas. All those
things I'd struggled to keep down for so long were okay after all.
It made me feel free.

It was only some time after he'd gone that I realised he'd neglected
to return my shadow. It was getting cold and I felt sure I'd need it.
It was annoying falling for a cheap trick.

## The White Rose
*(i.m. members of the White Rose German resistance movement)*

To think when thought is forbidden.
To love when taught to hate.
To resist the surge of the crowd.
To manoeuvre in a world of control.
To speak when silence is enforced.
To question when orders are the norm.
To look the tyrant in the eye and defy.
To dream of peace in a world of war.
To cradle hope newborn in your arms.
To feel the undertow and keep swimming.
To wait for the knock on the door.
To listen to the scrape of gaolers' keys.
To face down the ranting judge.
To listen for the drop of the blade.

**Berlin Zoo**


None of the animals knew why they were in the Zoo.
None of them knew why the Jewish people stopped
coming. They were very ignorant and couldn't read
the signs all around them. None of the animals liked
the sound of the air-raid warnings and in any case
could not take cover. All of the animals were afraid of
bombs landing and buildings collapsing all around.
Knautschke, the hippo, barely escaped the fire in his
compound. None of the animals understood why
the bombers were trying to kill them, night after night.
Most of the animals died without knowing why they
were in the firing line. When the Red Army attacked
the Zoo Tower was one of the final battlefields. None
of the animals knew why the artillery fell on them.
There were 3,175 animals in the Zoo. By May 1945
there were 91 left alive. In the end there were even
fewer since some were eaten by Red Army soldiers.

**Irma's Apple** *(SS Guard Bergen-Belsen, 1945)*

Irma Grese eats a juicy apple; places before the eyes
of a starving boy the generous core onto the floor.

It sits between the paws of her German Shepherd,
guarded by its jaws. She goes out, returns a little later.

Disappointed to see he had not attempted to get
the fruit she grinds it into a pulp under her boot.

**Sophie's Dream**
*(i.m. Sophie Scholl 9 May 1921 – 22 February 1943)*


You carry the infant close to you — careful not to fall;
wrapped in a shawl gazing out at the world the baby's
unfocussed eyes absorb the blur of everything. Hands
with tiny transparent fingernails on tiny fingers flex
the air in exploration. It's a fine sunny day, almost
festive, as you climb up the steep track to the church
that stands crag-like within its mountainous home.
Its plain wind-battered stones create a welcome
retreat for weary souls seeking refuge from the storm.

Before you a crevasse opens in slack jawed brutality;
its slippery edge gapes between you and your refuge.
An icy breath freezes all motion as you get nearer.
Just in time you place the child on the other side;
it lies among the flourishing buds of the future.
But it is too late for you and you fall into the abyss
that opens ever wider to swallow you. You know
Freisler's crooked blade will fall but your short
life burned so bright still we need to shield our eyes.


Note: this poem is based on the dream Sophie Scholl had the night before her execution, which she related to her cell mate Else Gebel the following morning. Sophie Scholl, aged 21, was executed on 22 February 1943 by guillotine for her role in the peaceful White Rose anti-Nazi resistance movement in Munich. She was sentenced to death (along with her brother Hans and Christoph Probst) by Hitler's ranting judge Roland Freisler who later became even more infamous for his role in the show trials of people involved in the failed assassination attempt on Hitler.